RELIGION

GORDON PLANEDIN

Copyright © 2024 by Gordon Planedin
ISBN: 978-1-77883-426-4 (Paperback)

All rights reserved. No part of this publication may be reproduced, distributed, or transmitted in any form or by any means, including photocopying, recording, or other electronic or mechanical methods, without the prior written permission of the author, except in the case brief quotations embodied in critical reviews and other noncommercial uses permitted by copyright law.

This publication contains the opinions and ideas of its author. It is intended to provide helpful and informative material on the subjects addressed in the publication. The author specifically disclaims all responsibility for any liability, loss, or risk, personal or otherwise, which is incurred as a consequence, directly or indirectly, of the use and application of any of the contents of this book.

BookSide Press
877-741-8091
www.booksidepress.com
orders@booksidepress.com

The Ten Commandments

1. Thou shalt have no other gods before me.
2. Thou shalt not make unto thee any graven image.
3. Thou shalt not take the name of the Lord thy God in vain.
4. Remember the Sabbath day, to keep it holy.
5. Honour thy father and thy mother.
6. Thou shall not kill.
7. Thou shall not commit adultery.
8. Thou shall not steal.
9. Thou shall not bear false witness against thy neighbor.
10. Thou shall not covet.

-Exodus 20:1-7

Religion	Adherents	Percentage
Christianity	2.4 billion	31.40%
Islam	1.9 billion	24.00%
Hinduism	1.2 billion	15.40%
Secular/Nonreligious/Agnostic/Atheist	1.1 billion	14.10%
Buddhism	506 million	6.00%
Chinese traditional religions	394 million	5.00%
Ethnic religions	300 million	3.00%
African traditional religions	100 million	1.20%
Sikhism	26 million	0.30%
Spiritism	15 million	0.19%
Judaism	14.7 million	0.18%
Baha'i	7.0 million	0.09%
Jainism	4.2 million	0.05%
Shinto	4.0 million	0.05%
Cao Dai	4.0 million	0.05%
Zoroastrianism	2.6 million	0.03%
Tenrikyo	2.0 million	0.02%
Animism	1.9 million	0.02%
Neo-Paganism	1.0 million	0.01%
Unitarian Universalism	0.8 million	0.01%
Rastafari	0.6 million	0.007%
Total	7.79 billion	100.00%

THE LORD'S PRAYER

Our Father, who art in heaven,
Hallowed be thy Name;
Thy kingdom come.
Thy will be done,
On earth as it is in heaven.
Give us this day our daily bread;
And forgive us our trespasses,
As we forgive those who trespass against us;
And lead us not into temptation,
But deliver us from evil.

[For thine is the kingdom,
And the power, and the glory,
for ever and ever.]

Amen.
(See Matthew 6:9-13)

*To my sweetheart and beloved wife for the last 65 years,
Mary Planedin.*

*Also, to my grandson, Gordon Shaw, who was a major help
throughout the whole process.*

PREFACE

The purpose of writing this book is not to destroy the character or the good works of any religious order.

On the contrary we recognize the fact that if the world and its civilizations survive we will need the cooperation and help of all the religious orders.

Our main concerns are that there are too many alternate Gods amongst the orders and that the competition between them for the righteous people is not to the benefit of our civilizations or the future of the world and its great beauty and its many wonders. If they could concede that there might be only one God then they could work together for the coming good which the world greatly needs.

It is very obvious to everyone that we have a multitude of religious orders around the world and that most people have some type of religious belief. This would seem to imply that goodness and mercy would be scattered throughout the world and that there are many Gods around for people to worship.

However, the whole universe seems to be controlled by some power that is so great that it is far beyond our comprehension.

By and large the power seems to be of a benevolent nature to mankind which is good, so for our purposes we can call it "God".

It would be reasonable to assume that there is only one such power since if there were more there could be a conflict between them to decide who is in charge and that would be disastrous.

Then there was the expectation that God would provide us with a heaven on earth as a reward for our good deeds but the manner this would occur is not very clear.

Alas there are some who contend that this has already been done in that we have been given a heaven on earth and that God expects us as tenants to appreciate the gift and to take good care of it.

Obviously, we have been terrible as tenants as in our greed we do not look into the future and act accordingly.

But we shall leave that to the various groups already involved in that process as we have felt that there is a more pressing problem now: Religion.

Despite the fact that mankind is all made exactly identical we all try to worship a different God and live a different lifestyle in order to magnify that difference.

Everyone has the exact same features, one nose, a mouth, two eyes, two ears, two hands and two legs so that if you ever go to help your neighbour you can use two hands instead of just one.

We are all twin brothers from a different mother. All this seems to be lost when it comes to their religions which we shall discuss in the following pages.

If you had wondered why mankind is all built exactly the same then this is something to think about, maybe The Good Lord wanted mankind to be able to relate to each-other much better. In that regard we have been found wanting to a dire degree especially in the areas of Religion.

We have noted some of the major religions but most of the same faults exist throughout.

RELIGIONS

I am writing this book because I am concerned that we are destroying our world and what is the best way to save it. First we have to establish is who owns the world and therefore who should be involved in the decisions in its care and preservation.

There should be no question in anyone's mind that every inhabitant of the world from the time they are born until the time they die are free and equal owners and therefore entitled to share in its care and maintenance.

The problem is that all the decisions are being made by the electors and they are too often tainted by greed with no concern about the damage to the world and what is left to future generations.

I have proposed for years that the younger generations below the voting age should be allowed to assemble review panels to check out all proposals which could have any negative impact on our environment and obviously their decisions should have some teeth.

To be effective, we should have a review panel in every province and in every state and the youth should be very involved in setting the age category as well as its scope.

It is alas obvious that at this stage religions are greatly involved in the decisions that are made and that they also make mistakes. We should therefore check up on their impact on the major decisions that we end up with and how they affect the futures of everyone.

Below we will do brief reviews of a few of the major religions and some of the major concerns.

ISLAM

People praying at Ramadan night in Blue Mosque on July 19, 2012 in Istanbul, Turkey.

Muhammad is messenger of god
Second largest religion
1.8 million Followers, 24.9% of world population

Muslim believe in angels

Sunni Muslims 75%-90%
Shia Muslims 10%-20%

Disagreement over the successor to Muhammad
One God Baran

Religion

Sheikh Zayed Grand Mosque, Abu Dhabi

Prophets: Adam, Abraham, Moses, Jesus
Five daily prayers
Mosque Place of Worship

Fasting = from dawn to after sunset during the month of Ramadan to encourage nearness to God and think of the needy
Pilgrimage at least once in lifetime

JUDAISM

Vector hamsa hand and david star, candlestick and holy text ingot or Torah, orthodox Jew and pomegranate. Temple or church, book pile and honey Judaism religion symbols, Jewish religious sketch icons.

10th largest religion; 14.5 million to 17.4 million Headquarters Jerusalem

Scripture - Tanakh. Principles of faith 1 of 13 belief with perfect faith that the creator blessed be his name is the creator and guide of everything that has been created. He alone has made, does make, and will make all things.

Religion

Orthodox Jewish men in Tallit prayer shawls standing from before dawn for Shacharit sunrise prayer at the Western/Wailing Wall or Kotel, the holiest place in Judaism: Jerusalem Israel

HINDUISM

*KOLKATA, INDIA-SEPTEMBER 27, 2017:
Young Hindu Priest worshipping Goddess Durga under holy smoke,
Durga Puja festival ritual.*

Is an Indian religion

World third largest with 1.25 billion followers 15-16%
Maybe the world's oldest religion
Swami Vivekananda
Vaidika dharma a way of life

Religion

Statue of Hindu goddess in Kathmandu Nepal.

The Hindu religion does not claim one prophet and does not worship one God and is not really a religion more of a way of life.

Hindu traditionally revere a body of religious literature.

The Vedas Artha Livelihood + Wealth
Kāma Pleasure
Moksa Liberation

BUDDHISM

Seated Buddha in a Lotus Pose

World's fourth largest religion 520 million followers/7% world population

Buddha - the Awakened One

Four noble truths taking refuge in the Buddha the dharma and the Sangha observance of moral precepts.

Siddhartha Gautama

Religion

Novices monk vipassana meditation at front of Buddha statue

CONFUCIANISM

Yogyakarta, December 20, 2020.
The atmosphere of people worshiping at the ketandan temple. Pagoda is a holy place for followers of the Confucian religion or followers of the Tri Dharma

Ruism China is a system of thought and behaviour starting from China, basically described as tradition, a philosophy a humanistic religion a way of governing or simply a way of life, Confucianism developed from what was later called the hundred schools of thought the teaching of the Chinese philosopher Confucius.

Religion

Confucius statue. Located in Nanjing Confucius Temple, Nanjing City, Jiangsu Province, China.

There are a lot of religious people who believe that to get through the pearly gates they should dress in a certain fashion while so many others must make a special pilgrimage, wear special clothes etc. and so many others wear a turban or a special cap and other.

Hocus and Pocus and a question arises if that is not better replaced by how you have treated your fellow man and woman.

Since we have many concerns regarding our religions we can look at more serious problems that exist.

Most people do not realize that our world is basically a time bomb and the clock is ticking.

The problem is that too many countries have more than enough nuclear bombs so that they can destroy the world in a very short time.

The danger is that the either by accident or that some fanatic with aides could send off a nuclear weapon and thereby start a nuclear war.

There is talk that about 1962 JFK and Khrushchev had been engaged in talks about dismantling all nuclear weapons and in that manner removing that threat.

However, JFK was assassinated and that was the end of that.

It would be a wonderful thing if the nations would realize that all those weapons as well as all others could be remade into something useful and to remove the danger of the destruction of all.

The large warships could have the weaponry removed and be used to haul food for people who are starving for the food we throw away every year.

Large bombers could be refitted with water tanks and be awesome for fighting fires.

Many nations engage in war games so it would be wonderful if the nations could change into having peace games instead.

CHRISTIANITY

Christians are one of the most persecuted religious group in the world, especially in the Middle-East, North Africa and South and East Asia. In 2017, Open Doors estimated approximately 260 million Christians are subjected annually to "high, very high, or extreme persecution" with North Korea considered the most hazardous nation for Christians. In 2019, a report commissioned by the United Kingdom's Secretary of State of the Foreign and Commonwealth Office (FCO) to investigate global persecution of Christians found persecution has increased, and is highest in the Middle East, North America, India, China, North Korea, and Latin America, among others, and that it is global and not limited to Islamic states.

Christianity is the most popular of all religions in the world to almost 2 of them all.

The catholic church being about half of the Christian population but since they have been fluctuating through the years they are mixed up like a dog's breakfast to include the protestants as the next largest part among many of the smaller branches.

Then there have been the more spiritual Christians such as the Molokan and the Doukhobors who broke from the Russian Orthodox Church and maintained a close relationship with Quakers and many others who like them believe in pacifism.

The Doukhobors went a bit further in that in the year 1885 in three separate villages in Russia they piled up dry firewood and then stacked all their weapons on top and then on a synchronized time on St Peter's Day they burned them all.

This was not well received by the government and they were discriminated against because of that.

A few years later Queen Victoria gave them exemption from military service and at the turn of the century two shiploads of Doukhobors went to Canada and probably there is more of that religion in Canada then in Russia.

Christianity is a religion which is based on many fine principles and good deeds but maybe because of their fanatic beliefs in their religion they are willing to be hypocrites and take other people's lives as evidenced throughout the years.

Some examples are the Crusades of the mid centuries, the thirty year wars, the English civil war and their actions throughout the years.

These acts are all in contradiction of one of the commandments "Thou shalt not kill"

Most people do not realize that a lot of prominent people like presidents would like to see nuclear weapons disappear. Harry S Truman the one who authorized the use of the first 2 atomic bombs against Japan is one. Dwight D. Eisenhower at the end of his second term of Presidency cautioned "Beware of the war machine" and there are many other world leaders. We are seeing the slogan "make America great again" but it is time to raise the bar as what is necessary now is to try "make our world great" for everyone to live and enjoy again.

As time goes on it is becoming apparent that in order for the world to survive we have to make the world great again in order for nations to be great.

The vast majority of the people want mainly the basic needs in that they want to have a family with shelter, food and the basic necessities of life.

When they can have that then there is a hope for peace and for the world to be a happy place. Speaking of Religion and guns we shall touch on the second amendment.

When the founding fathers were forming the constitution and doing the amendments they included the second amendment to allow to citizens to bear arms they also encouraged them to do so for a very good reason.

At the time the country had only emerged and was surrounded by insecurity and enemies and to have armed citizens acting to help defend it was desirable and wise.

Gradually the weapons got better and better like the AK 45 5 and other assault weapons like the m16 which seemed right for the situation.

However there should have been the realization that a few million people equipped with assault rifles as a defense against an army with nuclear weapons wasn't worth a pinch of coonshit. So much for that idea.

Then there was the expectation that arose that they could protect everyone from an internal enemy but this was disapproved by the events in Jan 6/21 since it was impossible to tell friend from foe. Lots of traitors, liars and terrorists looked almost like American people.

For the reason it us plain to see that there is no use of them for anything in the future.

Therefore if anyone with half a brain would like to get rid of them they should sell them to the govt.

Regardless of how many lives we can save there could be many others benefits to be had.

At last the people would be able to convert their residence from a fortress to a home that it was supposed to be for living and loving and being able to relax and enjoy life again.

As for the second amendment, all that a person have to do is to take your jacket off and wear short sleeved shirt.

Conclusion: Assault rifles are useless in that concept.

And as for this reason for the greatness of America anyone with half a brain would admit that America's greatness came not from the fact that they have the most nuclear bombs or the greatest forces but in spite of that their greatness came because of empathy, their compassion a kindness it came from, "Give me your sick, your poor and your lame" and not only did they talk the talk but they walked the walk.

Some of the leaders while pioneering greatness only degraded the country thank God some of the greatness is returning.

The other big benefit the people would get would be that the family could use the extra money to spread about the family or maybe the husband could take his sweet on a weekend honeymoon to celebrate their freedom from guns.

There have been some very tragic situations with our weather in recent times and obviously much of that could be caused by the changes we have allowed to occur in our weather.

Also maybe we cannot help but wonder if some of it is an example of the wrath of God to punish mankind for their damage to our world.

I would like to at this time do an excerpt from Desiderata, 1927 "Therefore be at peace with God, whatever you conceive Him to be. And whatever your labors and aspirations, in the noisy confusion of life, keep peace in your soul. With all its sham, drudgery and broken dreams, it is still a beautiful world. Be cheerful. Strive to be happy."

I would suggest that everyone should have a full copy of Desiderata in their home.

We must agree that if our current leaders could then turn our swords into ploughshares we could have a wonderful world to live in.

In the meantime if you can live with only one God, only one Earth, only one civilization content to be twin brothers and sisters and if we can relate to our family and provide them with empathy, kindness and compassion, stay away from false prophets who would only provide us with lies and hatred we might be able to live in a wonderful world forever and ever. In closing I wish to remind people of someone saying many years ago "and as ye shall do unto the least of my brethren, likewise shall I do unto you." Amen.

SUMMARY

It is very puzzling that all of our elected officials gave an oath before their god to faithfully serve their country as their first loyalty is to their country, its government and their fellow man.

It causes one to wonder what kind of a God they worship, it must be a very forgiving God or maybe they had never heard the saying "Use not the name of your God in vain."

I would like to offer a world of advice to those who seem to have a small regard for honesty and a total disregard for any possibly consequences because of their actions.

"The Lord works in mysterious ways his wonders to perform."

You maybe can fool most of the people most of the time but no one can fool everyone every time. Take care as the chickens sometimes come home to roost.

A word of caution to the voters. Do not vote for liars and hypocrites as all they wish to do is destroy democracy & replace it with dictatorship.

The author and his wife both came from poor families, this made it easier to understand the problems that the less fortunate had. We had through the years tried to help in that regard and hope to continue that in the future. To this end, any profits that come from the sales of this book and the profits from the sale of Solomon Levi Mackeefer shall be transmitted to a special account to be used only for charity.

www.ingramcontent.com/pod-product-compliance
Lightning Source LLC
LaVergne TN
LVHW041552060526
838200LV00037B/1252